In this series –

RUMI READINGS
FOR
ADDICTION

RUMI READINGS
FOR
ADDICTION

JALALUDDIN RUMI

The Scheherazade Foundation

The Scheherazade Foundation CIC
85 Great Portland Street
London
W1W 7LT
United Kingdom
www.SF.Charity
info@SF.Charity

First published by The Scheherazade Foundation CIC, 2025

RUMI READINGS FOR ADDICTION

A CIP catalogue record for this title is available from the British Library.

ISBN 978-1-915311-83-2

Introduction

Jalaluddin Rumi was born in Balkh, Afghanistan, in the year 1207, and died in Konya, Turkey, in 1273.

During the sixty-six years spanning this pair of dates, he produced a range of extraordinary work in Persian which, today, is classed as 'Sufi Mysticism'.

In the seven and a half centuries since his death, Rumi's corpus, which includes *The Masnavi* and *Fihi Ma Fihi*, has been circulated widely across the Near East, the Arab world, and Central Asia.

Generations of students continue to commit selections of the 60,000 verses to heart, and allow Rumi's way of thought to permeate through all areas of their lives.

Although Orientalists venturing eastward from Europe in the 1700s occasionally made note of Sufi Mysticism, they tended to witness it through the more theatrical frills – such as 'whirling dervishes' – rather than through a deep appreciation of the texts.

It wasn't until the close of the nineteenth century that the first wholescale translations of Rumi's written work began to appear in Europe.

Even then, they remained very much the purview of a few academics, whose translations were – even for the time – laden with indescribably floral and cumbersome prose.

Although in the Occident, students would find themselves scrutinizing Rumi's corpus, it wasn't until more recently that accessible appreciations of his work became available.

A few years before his death, I asked my father – the Sufi scholar and thinker Idries Shah – for his thoughts on Rumi's legacy in the West.

Sitting in his favourite chair, a porcelain cup of green tea in hand, he looked at me hard.

'I never cease to be amazed,' he said.

'Amazed by what?'

'By the way people don't take what's perfectly packaged, and ready and waiting for them, but rather obsess with something else.'

'With what?'

'With endless and nonsensical trimmings, trappings, and paraphernalia.'

My father sipped his tea.

After a moment of silent thought, he continued:

'Read Rumi in the original Persian,' he said, 'and so delicate are the verses that you have tears rolling down your cheeks. Yet here in the West, it's served up as something submerged in a thick, glutinous gravy, so much so that its utterly inedible.'

I reminded my father that a series of publications had recently found their way to press – publications that presented Rumi's couplets in an utterly new way.

Stripped bare of what my father had referred to as 'gravy', they were light.

Indeed, they were lighter than light.

My father rolled his eyes at the thought.

'In any other place, and at any other time,' he said, 'people would be up in arms. Or, if they weren't, they'd be laughing until their sides split. Imagine it – Western poets with absolutely no knowledge of the original Persian text touting new, bestselling editions of Rumi's work! It's what we call "The Soup of the Soup of the Soup".'

In the years since my father's death, Occidental society has been flooded with all things Rumi.

Couplets ascribed to him are read solemnly at weddings across the United States, Europe, and beyond.

Wisdom drawn from his poetry is tattooed daily over the backs and limbs of Hollywood A-listers.

But the precious words uttered at weddings, tattooed into skin, and quoted in abundance, hold little or no bearing to the original verses of Jalaluddin Rumi.

So, there it is…

The great Sufi Master's wisdom available:

(a) in a form that's unreadable because it's all covered in glutinous gravy, or

(b) in another form that's completely distorted – the Soup of the Soup of the Soup.

One thing that *is* evident is that the West can benefit enormously from a clean, clear rendition of Rumi's thinking – as the East has done over the last seven hundred years.

For this reason, we have commissioned entirely new translations, gleaned in particular from *The Masnavi*. Selected and translated by native Persian-speaking scholars, the emphasis has been on maintaining the lightness of Rumi's poetry.

In an age of relentless speed and digital overload, and so as to allow the work to be accessed by those who may benefit from it most, we have arranged a series of bite-sized morsels by way of theme.

We encourage you to do what students, scholars, and ordinary people have done across the East for centuries...

To pick a single couplet, or a handful – and to read them over and over, allowing them to seed themselves in your mind.

Little by little, having taken root, they will blossom and bear fruit.

Tahir Shah

How to Use This Book

Rumi Readings for Addiction

This book is not a cure. It is not a replacement for professional treatment, support groups, or loved ones. But it *is* something else. It is a companion – a gentle, non-judging voice drawn from centuries past, yet speaking directly to the hidden chambers of the heart today.

The words in these pages come from Jalaluddin Rumi, one of the world's great spiritual poets, mystics, and psychologists of the soul. Translated directly from the original Persian by scholars rooted in Rumi's own tradition, they have been carefully selected and arranged with one purpose: **to offer support, insight, and perspective to those living with addiction – and those who care for them**.

Whether you are actively struggling, in recovery, watching a loved one suffer, or simply searching for healing of some kind, this book offers a space to pause, breathe, and feel seen.

An Invitation, Not an Instruction

Rumi's poems are not rules to follow. They do not tell you what to do or who to be. They are more like open windows. Each one lets in a little more light, a little more air – sometimes warm, sometimes sharp, sometimes unexpected.

You do not need to read this book all at once. In fact, it may be more powerful if you don't.

Instead, take it slowly. One quote at a time. One breath at a time.

Let it meet you where you are.

A Poetic Companion on the Road to Recovery

Addiction is not simply a matter of habits or substances. It is about pain. About disconnection. About the unbearable tension between what we long for and what we fear. Rumi, writing over 700 years ago, understood this tension. He lived through loss, longing, love, and ecstatic confusion. He knew what it meant to be broken – and to find meaning inside that brokenness.

His words are not about fixing you. They are about revealing what is already whole beneath the wound.

This book is divided into ten parts, each addressing a different facet of the addiction experience – from the origins of craving to the surrender of the self, from the pain of loss to the flicker of joy. You may move through them in order, or open to the part that feels most relevant today.

There is no right way to use this book.

There is only *your* way.

Read One Quote at a Time

One of the most grounding ways to use this book is to read a **single quote per day** – perhaps in the morning, or at a quiet moment in the evening. Read it slowly. Out loud if you can. Let it echo a little.

Then close the book.

Let the quote work on you without effort. You may understand it, or not. It may resonate, or not. That's all part of the process.

Some quotes are gentle. Others might sting. Some may seem confusing. Don't worry. Rumi speaks to different parts of us at different times. What feels distant today may feel life-saving tomorrow.

Let the Quote Find You

You can also use this book more intuitively. Let it fall open. Let your eye land somewhere. Trust that what appears is what you need.

This is how mystics and seekers have read sacred texts for centuries – not as linear stories, but as **living guidance**. If a quote startles you, touches you, or makes you uncomfortable, pause there. Ask why. Sit with it. Let it deepen.

Bring It Into the Body

Rumi's words are not just for the mind. They are for the body, too – the place where trauma lives, where cravings arise, and where healing begins.

Try reading a quote, then closing your eyes. Notice how your body feels. What changes? Where does the quote land – in your chest? Your stomach? Your breath?

This is not analysis. This is presence.

Reflect, Journal, Repeat

Many people find it helpful to keep a notebook or journal alongside this book. You might write down a quote and respond to it. Ask questions. Let it prompt memories. Or just write what you're feeling, even if it has nothing to do with the quote.

Rumi's words are not demanding. They simply want to be in the room with you.

Over time, you may notice a shift. Not a dramatic transformation, but something quieter – a softening, a widening, a sense that you are not alone inside your struggle.

Share It, If You Can

If you feel safe doing so, consider reading a quote with someone else – a therapist, a sponsor, a friend, or a group. Rumi was not a solitary figure. His poetry was born in community, in conversation, in spiritual companionship.

Sometimes just one line shared aloud can open a door between people that has long been closed.

Remember What You Already Know

Addiction can feel like amnesia – a forgetting of your own strength, your own clarity, your own worth. Rumi's voice is here to **remind** you, not to teach you something new.

He writes: '*The mirror of the soul only reflects clearly when it has been polished by both longing and humility.*'

The mirror does not judge what it reflects – it simply reveals. In the same way, recovery is not about becoming someone else. It is about seeing yourself more clearly, with compassion, with truth, and with less distortion. Longing and humility – the ache to heal, and the courage to admit your need – are not signs of weakness. They are the polish that slowly, patiently, brings you back to the light of your own being.

Final Thought

This is not a book about being fixed. It is a book about becoming real.

Real with your fear. Real with your joy. Real with the fact that sometimes you don't know what's next – and that's okay.

Rumi never asks you to be perfect. Only to keep walking.

Part 1

On the Nature of Addiction

1

For such a paltry sum,
what sort of transaction is this –
bartering the soul for a fistful of dust?

2

O wise rescuer,
no one wills until You will it.
From You stem both the seeking
and the kindness.
Who are we to declare?
you are both the beginning and the end.

3

Despite appearing as adversaries and contradictions, day and night intertwine to form a unified reality.

4

Even if my outward demeanour seems bitter,
it is only that
my heart rejoices inwardly
by divine decree.
A parent's innocent gaze
shields their child from harm.

5

Those who find the path to enlightenment
through solitude
do not rely on external sources or knowledge.
Their vision transcends ordinary knowledge,
surpassing the mundane world.

6

Despite the capture of my teacher's bird
by the master's trap,
I wholeheartedly dedicated myself to them,
experiencing a state of euphoria
and carefree joy in their service.

7

If you are watchful and awake,
you will see the response to your actions
in every moment.

8

How can blossoms turn into knots,
when flowers shine like armour?
Fruits emerge as blossoms fade;
even when the body weakens,
the spirit can still soar.

9

Giving up lust, greed, and wrath
is a sign of prophetic virtue and nobility.
Difficulties surround paradise,
while desires encircle hellfire.

10

Pain is a valuable experience,
for it conceals numerous blessings within,
as the shell of a walnut or almond
encases its delicate and delicious core.

Part 2
The Inner Struggle

11

The path to happiness often winds through valleys of sorrow,
laying the foundation for moments of joy.
Sorrow cleans and clears,
sweeping away the dust of despair from life's abode,
making space for the blossoming joy of compassion.

12

Virtue is naturally attracted to goodness;
wickedness is inherently associated with evil.
Be aware!
For bitterness will always align with bitterness.
When will deception ever be united with Truth?

13

They thought about their actions towards others,
and faced the consequences imposed by life.
I wanted to incite jealousy in others,
but instead, they approached me,
and fell into a well.

14

When you sincerely place your trust in someone,
this door of yours opens to numerous accomplishments.
A single coin becomes multiplied by four,
and one adversary transforms into a group of four.

15

A fatigued and debilitated sheep fell behind.
Moses, the divinely chosen one,
brushed the dust off it.
He tenderly caressed its back and head,
offering comfort and attention,
just like a mother.

16

Avoid complacency with falsehood,
for neither water nor oil can extinguish its flame.

17

A friend serves as a reflection of the soul
during times of sadness.
Would you intentionally blur a mirror
by breathing on it?
To prevent it from concealing itself,
you must control each and every one of your breaths.

18

Hope emerges from the depths of sorrow,
and a vision emerges from the heart
during the darkest moments.

19

If the incense within you ignites,
the universe will be filled with gentle fragrance.
You are neither the incense consumed by flames
nor the spirit trapped by sorrow.
Incense ignites through separation from the flame,
yet the wind cannot alter the essence of light.

20

Without imperfections,
how could the value of gold be demonstrated?
Those who acknowledge and understand
their own deficiencies
move closer to their ideal state.

Part 3
Illusion and Reality

21

It is confusion,
not this nor that.
The riches must be sought after;
this is destruction.
You lose the true treasure
because of a delusion
that you mistake for a treasure.

22

The heart experiences peace
through honest expression,
as the thirsty find comfort in water.

23

As life proves profoundly intoxicating,
guilt dissipates from the heart
and reason from the mind.
For millennia, humanity has been led astray
by this intoxication of existence.

24

Wisdom is able to distinguish
between similarities and differences,
and is not easily influenced
by superficial appearance.

25

You are not merely an individual, dear friend;
you embody the universe
and a vast, deep ocean.

26

Feel the love that ignites within this heart
for the Beloved when it strikes.
The more God's love permeates your essence,
the more certain it becomes that God loves you.

27

Because it draws you nearer to the friend,
thankfulness is the essence of blessings,
while blessings are merely their outer layer.

28

While I stopped trying,
my heart remained restless;
though everyone else gave up,
their spirit never found a moment of rest.
Those who commit themselves
to mastering a particular skill
will ultimately succeed.
But the highest level of mastery
is attained by those who strive
for improvement without cease.

29

Do not focus on the yellowing leaves of the tree;
rather, harvest its apples, for they are ripe.
Do the yellow leaves lack meaning?
They signify maturity and wholeness.

30

Within the realms exist both sorrowful,
shadowy souls and pure, radiant spirits.
These entities differ vastly from one another;
while one harbours a precious pearl,
the other possesses a mere semblance of one.
The world was fashioned with the intent of revelation,
ensuring that the hidden treasures of wisdom
remain unearthed.

Part 4
Seeking Guidance

31

Trials become sweet when you perceive clarity,
and medicine becomes pleasurable
when health is restored.

32

I observed the house with its many adornments,
and was disturbed by my intense desire to own it.
The wise man remarked,
'You are like a child surrounded
by an abundance of decorations.'

33

Do not weave webs of deception
and manipulation in your mind,
for success does not favour the crafty.

34

If seeking affirmation,
turn not away from the sun,
for it has arrived.

35

The heart guides you towards others
who possess compassion and empathy,
while the physical body limits you to matters
pertaining to the material world.

36

Those who live indulgently will meet a painful end;
those who venerate the corporeal will not redeem the spirit.

37

Lament the cruel companion!
Lament!
Find yourselves a reputable partner,
O beloved people.

38

The blind Pharaoh thought the sea was dry,
and so he advanced with might and power.
On entering, he was engulfed by a single droplet,
and his face was perpetually obscured.

39

God gives dust and precious stones
amazing colours and qualities,
making little souls fight over them.
Children long for the bread
that they create from dough shaped
like camels and lions.
They will not believe you,
even if you tell them the truth.

40

On seeing his arrogance,
the Grand Mufti simply attributed some
responsibility to the person for the rebellion.
He criticized him for his excessive pursuit of profit,
even taking liberties, like cutting a portion of
a cypress tree without permission.
Where is your focus and reason,
O wine-drinker,
that you perceive knowledge as an adversary?
He noted that using offensive language
reflects one's character,
and that attitude can influence one's appearance.
Countenance should be like an unyielding iron surface,
candidly revealing even the sight of an unattractive face.

Part 5
Suffering & Surrender

41

True existence is found in death and hardship;
the essence of life lies hidden in mystery.

42

O seeker,
your companion is your clarity of vision:
make sure it remains unclouded by dust and debris.
Be mindful;
speak in a manner that avoids harm or confusion;
refrain from letting unnecessary information
obscure your clarity.

43

His hidden kindness lies within His wrath;
surrendering your life to Him will elevate your soul.
Abandon doubt and deceit;
move forward, for He has called you to ascend.

44

Examine your essence to discern its goodness;
this understanding underpins the core of religious teachings.
By delving inward, you can better grasp
your personal identity,
your values and ideals as an individual.

45

A beggar in our midst stirs the wine,
and our minds spin the wheel.
It is we who become drunk,
not the wine itself;
it is we who give life to the form,
not the other way around.

46

He asked,
'What wisdom lies in life and its mysteries
when the pure essence is confined in this shadowy realm?'
Clear water is hidden in the mud;
the pure soul is trapped within bodily form.

47

O you who are the mirror of royal beauty,
O you who are the heavenly script,
everything that is in the world is within you.
Look within for what you seek,
because you are everything.

48

Even as Gabriel offers aid,
you stand guard like a brother.

49

As a sail appears weightless above a ship,
so love becomes eternal when reciprocated.
Step closer to the young child
who instinctively pulls away to avoid falling over.

50

O noble ones,
this world is like a tree,
and we are like its immature fruits.

Part 6

The Role of Awareness

51

When something lingers for an extended time,
it is sometimes seen as the fruit of boredom.
Was it the victim of its own actions,
or merely deceptive perception?

52

Whatever you say or reveal,
you only add another layer of concealment.

53

It transcends categorization,
methodology, and moderation;
neither attached nor detached,
O Perfection.
By Your grace,
O admirable one,
we float in life's waters like fish.

54

No one dies with remorse about dying itself;
their sole lament is that death arrived too soon.
They descended from a well into expansive plains
amidst prosperity, joy and contentment.

55

Disregard the insignificant acts of rudeness,
and choose to forgive without seeking revenge.
Pledge that you would not entertain thoughts of division,
but instead exert effort towards unity and reuniting.

56

All things, including the air we breathe
and the words uttered by magicians,
are part of God's creation.
Without uttering a single word,
God's allure communicates a hundred secret meanings
through cause and effect.

57

Upon my birth, I emerged from a confined existence
into a realm of vibrant and exhilarating atmosphere.
I perceived the universe as a womb until this moment,
when, amidst the flames, I saw tranquillity.

58

See the mind as illumination,
your desire as greed and longing.
These two only obscure and bewilder,
while mind serves
as the source of enlightenment.

59

You are the one who inflicts wounds upon yourself;
in that instant, you condemn your own existence.

60

When the air is not fresh,
faith too begins to lose its freshness.
The key to that locked door won't turn
through desire alone.

Part 7
Healing Through Love

61

Those who reach unity
express it in stillness.
Their mouths remain silent
while their eyes, turned from the world,
reveal the beauty within.

62

Those who embark on the path without a guide
may turn a two-day trip
into a journey of a hundred years.
Anyone who rushes to the Kaaba
without proper guidance
will become disoriented and embarrassed,
and wander aimlessly.

63

There are many deceitful people;
be cautious about extending your hand to everyone.

64

You have nothing but what you strive for;
the worth of effort lies in striving for what you want.
The Lord is the greatest giver of effort;
indeed, no one of low status is a part
of the kingdom of effort.

65

I assume the role of his vision, dexterity, and emotions in order to protect his wealth from mistaken direction.

66

Among the fakirs,
assess them carefully,
and choose the one
who is truly genuine.

67

Unfit for the palace in their raw state,
the unripe cling steadfastly to the branch.
Their grip loosens as they ripen,
acquiring a delightful flavour.

68

Its joy is a by-product
of the fading of pleasure in the world,
be it a drink or a meal.
It was enjoyable and grew pleasurable,
even if it lost its effectiveness due to enjoyment.

69

The elderly gentleman of summer
and the youngsters of July
contrast sharply.
The youth may embody the darkness of the night,
while the elderly person shines
with the luminosity of the moon.

70

Well-chosen words have the power to ignite an unlit lamp,
like a lit lamp kissing an extinguished
one with its own flame.

Part 8

The Journey to Wholeness

71

As your eyes close,
sorrow curls around you.
How can the distant radiance of the eye be seen?
If you feel sorrow, even while fully aware,
know that the innermost core of your being,
the seat of intuition
and understanding,
is asleep.
Wake it gently.

72

When truth is illuminated by peace,
the heart does not rely on false words.

73

Human beings may be compared to trees,
with their agreements like roots.
It is crucial to exert effort in nurturing
and caring for these roots.

74

Actions that originate from your heart and soul
should be embraced and cherished,
just as you would cradle your own child.

75

An adversary is one who intends harm,
rather than inflicting harm upon himself.
A bat does not threaten the sun;
instead, it is its own enemy,
hiding in shadows.

76

Look within and abandon fruitless searching;
search inside yourself rather than
constantly seeking validation from others.

77

I was drunk
and asked my teacher to give me
clear understanding
of existence and non-existence.
He replied,
telling me to leave,
and that by distancing myself
from the tribulations of others,
I would discover peace.

78

What is life?
It is recognizing right from wrong,
celebrating compassion,
and mourning when bad things happen.
Being aware of things is the essence of life;
so become more aware
if you want to be more alive.

79

Though I may travel and explore distant lands,
how can my love for my homeland
ever fade from my heart?

80

Though you appear as a microcosm,
in your essence
you are the macrocosm.

Part 9
Transformation & Renewal

81

Remain on solid ground,
and do not venture into the depths of the ocean.
Stay content by the water's edge and speak sparingly.

82

On spinning around and feeling dizzy,
it may seem as though the building is rotating,
but it is, in fact, you who are in motion.

83

We are the echoes of our deeds,
and the universe is like a mountain
upon which they reverberate.

84

The struggle of the soul persists until death separates us.
Perfection is the only path to reaching the summit.

85

When you see a mirage in the distance,
you instinctively rush towards it,
only to realize that you are captivated
by your own illusion.

86

There exists a fundamental connection
between soil, water, and flowers:
God infused life and emotion into each of them.

87

Life is obscured by the facade of death,
and death is embedded within the core of life.

88

The divine spirit proclaims:
'Do not despair,'
like a father searching for his lost son,
looking in every place.

89

Having forgotten the shape
he materialized,
a storm tore inside him.
His fists landed on his face
and head as he banged his skull
on the door and the wall.

90

To know one's identity
on the Day of Judgement
is the essence of all knowledge.

Part 10
Freedom & Transcendence

91

Simply put, a friend's face is the mirror of the soul:
a reflection of who they truly are.

92

O son,
each person's death reflects their true essence:
to the enemy, it is an enemy;
and to the friend, it is a friend.
What you fear as death rising above
is merely your fear of yourself.
Be aware, O soul.

93

Is there a calligrapher
who would write a line beautifully
just for the line's own sake,
without regard to how it reads?
The design appears to be for an unknown reason,
and it is closed for an additional unknown purpose.
Not only for aesthetic appeal and visual exhibition,
but also, for the sake of reading, do calligraphers write.

94

Fortunate is the person
who acknowledges their own shortcomings,
for those who criticize faults in others
often find those very flaws reflected back on themselves.
Half of these issues stem from their own errors,
while the other half arise from what is imperceptible.
If you have ten wounds on your head,
you must tend to them yourself.

95

Cursed is the one
whose thoughts are focused solely on material matters,
whose repulsive soul is forceful and on guard.
Their mind is inevitably overpowered,
and their words yield only detriment.

96

He lost consciousness and bowed his head
upon arriving at the perfumers' market.
The tanner, who was his brother,
swiftly and cleverly made his way to the designated spot,
taking immediate action.
He kept his distance from others to shield them
from noticing his condition.
Discreetly, he shared confidential information with him,
then gently placed an object on his forehead.

97

I direct my gaze not towards you,
but rather towards the depths of your heart;
I present a gift to her,
the essence of my being.
I am in the same position as you
when it comes to being with her;
the skies are beneath the feet of our mothers.

98

The world, veiled in desire, deceives the senses,
leading astray those who succumb to its allure.

99

The essence of life comes solely from
experiences and challenges;
those with greater knowledge possess
a deeper understanding of existence.

100

The soul frequently remains asleep behind a shroud,
as you have yet to unveil the authentic nature of death.
Until there is death, the complete spirit cannot manifest;
without wholeness, ascension to greatness is unattainable.

Finis

www.ingramcontent.com/pod-product-compliance
Lightning Source LLC
Chambersburg PA
CBHW020451100426
42813CB00031B/3328/J